Life's *Spiritual* Instruction Book

An inspirational collection
of 500 ideas for daily living

by

Dr. David Huddleston

6-13-98

Mom -

I know you'd really enjoy + appreciate this book - That is why I got it for you. Congratulations on acheiving your goal! You are an awesome role model + I cannot fully express how happy + proud I am of you. Way to go + good luck in the future!!

♡ Alinita.

Published by Maranatha Ministries International

First Printing 1994
Second Printing 1995
Third Printing 1998

Cover design by Edie Huddleston

ISBN 0-9640922-0-4

Printed in the United States of America.

Introduction

THE FOLLOWING five hundred hints, admonitions, and exhortations were originally given to my son and daughter as they were preparing to leave the nest and go off to college and into the "real world" which lay just beyond our front door. In trying to prepare them in some small way, I have also sought to make the Bible come alive by providing supporting scripture references for each entry. I have always believed the Bible to be an

• Introduction •

intensely practical book and I have tried to ensure that all my suggestions are Biblically based. I hope that the reader will receive a blessing which will prove to be of some practical value in his or her daily life.

Dr. David Huddleston

For my son, Sean, and my daughter, Heather,
who have taught (and are still teaching)
me how to be a father.

1 • Be humble.

2 • Try to be kind to everyone you meet because they're probably having a hard time with life.

3 • Make it your practice to be a peacemaker.

4 • Be careful what you look at. Make a covenant with your eyes.

5 • Refrain from swearing.

6 • Don't seek revenge from those who hurt you.

7 • Say a prayer for anyone who offends you.

8 • When you give to the needy, do it anonymously.

9 • Say your prayers. God already knows your needs, but you honor him by asking.

10 • Be careful what you say. What is said can never be unsaid.

11 • Use the gifts that God has given you to your best ability.

12 • There is more happiness in giving than there is in receiving.

13 • Learn to forgive.

14 • Don't be materialistic.

15 • Don't worry. It doesn't help.

16 • Don't be judgmental.

17 • Remember the Golden Rule.

18 • Avoid people who tell you that they know what God's will is for you.

19 • Be a hearer and a doer of the Word.

20 • Be shrewd in your dealings with the world, but innocent in your motives.

21 • Show hospitality to those in need.

22 • Be reconciled (and make amends) with those whom you have hurt.

23 • You can tell a tree by the fruit it bears. You can tell what kind of person someone is by the good (or bad) that he or she does.

24 • Tell your mother you love her.

25 • Practice self-discipline.

26 • Live your life so as not to be ashamed of anything you do.

27 • Pay your taxes.

28 • Don't let pride get in your way when it comes to doing the right thing.

29 • Get rid of anything that causes you to do something that you know is wrong.

30 • Remember that we are accountable to God for everything we say and do.

31 • When you need some advice, ask a Christian.

32 • Forgive everyone so that you can be forgiven.

33 • Be aware that rich people seldom sense their personal need of God as readily as others do.

34 • What may seem impossible to you is still possible with God.

35 • Don't be misled by the (lack of) moral standards of the world. It is irrelevant.

36 • God's grace is boundless.

37 • God is sovereign and he is in charge.

38 • Be willing to serve.

39 • Remember that God always answers our prayers. Sometimes he says, "Yes," sometimes he says, "No," and sometimes he says, "Not yet."

40 • Christ's first and greatest commandment is, "Love the Lord your God with all your heart and with all your soul and with all your mind."

41 • Christ's second commandment is,
"Love your neighbor as yourself."

42 • Give all you can afford to your church.

43 • If you see people who are hungry,
buy them a meal.

44 • If you know of people who are sick,
visit them.

45 • When you pray, ask for God's will to be done.

46 • Share your faith with someone when you have a chance.

47 • Remember that men and women are equal in God's sight.

48 • Understand that the fruit of the Spirit is love, joy, peace, patience, kindness, goodness, faithfulness, gentleness, and self-control. Try to let other people see these qualities in you.

49 • Carry another person's burdens and you'll help yourself as well.

50 • Never forget that God has chosen you for a very special purpose in life. The key is to find out what it is.

51 • Pray for discernment. It is a good thing to have.

52 • Remember that faith is God's gift to us, not our gift to God.

53 • Be at peace with God.

54 • Try to be even-tempered. Someone once said, "Who the devil would destroy, he first makes angry."

55 • When the time comes for you to get married, remember that the key to a happy marriage is to submit to one another out of reverence for Christ.

56 • Be considerate of other people's needs.

57 • Whatever you do, do it without complaining or arguing.

58 • Persevere. It is a sign of maturity.

59 • Don't be anxious about anything. It only makes it worse.

60 • Remember that people live in their own thought world. So concentrate on whatever is good and right.

61 • Learn to be content in whatever circumstances you find yourself.

62 • It is pleasing to God to give your money to missionaries.

63 • Ask God to fill you with the knowledge of his will through all spiritual wisdom and understanding.

64 • Don't hold a grudge.

65 • Make it your ambition to lead a quiet life that others will respect.

66 • Stay alert and self-controlled.

67 • Encourage those who are not as strong
as you are and be patient with them.

68 • Be happy!

69 • Learn to be thankful for whatever
happens.

70 • Test everything and hold on to what is good.

71 • Don't quench the Spirit.

72 • Don't ever get tired of doing what is right.

73 • Be at peace with everyone.

74 • Don't be a lover of money. It is not money itself, but the love of money that is the problem.

75 • Avoid conceited people.

76 • Guard your reputation jealously.

77 • Keep a clear conscience. You'll sleep better.

78 • It is a good thing to stay in good physical condition. Be sure to keep spiritually fit as well.

79 • Don't let anyone intimidate you because you are young.

80 • Treat older people with kindness and respect.

81 • When you compete as an athlete, play according to the rules.

82 • Meditate on God's Word regularly. It really helps.

83 • Pursue faith, love, and peace.

84 • Don't have anything to do with stupid arguments.

85 • Don't resent those who are trying to teach you.

86 • Remember that there is a reward for everyone who looks forward to Jesus' return.

87 • Love what is good. There will never be enough of it.

88 • When dealing with divisive people, warn them twice and after that don't have anything to do with them.

89 • Tell somebody about Jesus and what he has done for you.

90 • Encourage someone who needs it (everyone does).

91 • Don't work or shop on Sunday if you can help it.

92 • Remember that faith is being sure of what we hope for and certain of what we do not see.

93 • The "Big Bang" theory is not consistent with God's Word.

94 • Understand that the universe was made at God's command so that what is seen was not made out of what was visible.

95 • Don't be discouraged when you have to endure a hardship. Just remember that the Lord disciplines those he loves.

96 • Make every effort to live a life of holiness. It's what God expects of us.

97 • Be sure to show hospitality to strangers. You never know who they might be.

98 • Be content with the things you have and don't covet what others have.

99 • Share what you have with those less fortunate.

100 • Obey those who are in positions of authority and pray for them.

101 • Remember that when your faith is tested (count on it), the testing develops perseverance which leads to spiritual maturity.

102 • Be quick to listen.

103 • Be slow to speak.

104 • Be slow to become angry.

105 • Guard against self-deception.

106 • Never refuse help to an orphan or widow.

107 • God's environmentalists are those who keep themselves from being polluted by the world.

108 • God identifies with the not-so-rich-and-famous.

109 • Faith must be accompanied by action.

110 • The fear of God is the beginning of wisdom.

111 • Resist the devil and he will run away from you.

112 • Come near to the Lord and he will come near to you.

113 • If you know the right thing to do and don't do it, it is just as bad as doing the wrong thing.

114 • There is a special danger in affluence because it leads to a false sense of security.

115 • Slow down and take time to enjoy today.

116 • The prayers of a good-hearted person are strong medicine.

117 • Trust God.

118 • The real "beautiful people" are those with a quiet and gentle spirit.

119 • Don't repay an insult with an insult.

120 • Love covers over many errors.

121 • Jesus was a real person in time and space and history.

122 • The Lord knows how to help you when you feel hopeless. He's in the miracle business.

123 • A person is a slave to whatever has mastered him or her.

124 • Never hesitate to give money to Christians who are having financial problems.

125 • Jesus knows all about how you are feeling right now.

126 • We love the Lord because he first loved us.

127 • If you ask God anything according to his will, he will hear you.

128 • Guard against self-absorption.

129 • You will find petty dictators in every church who consider themselves indispensable. Learn to deal with them in love.

130 • Try to imitate what is good.

131 • Don't hesitate to show mercy to those who don't agree with you.

132 • Don't be known as a "lukewarm Christian."

133 • Your prayers are like sweet incense to God.

134 • Pay no attention to anyone who believes in astrology.

135 • Avoid fortune tellers.

136 • Once in your life, teach a Sunday school class.

137 • Don't be surprised someday if God sends an angel to speak to you (they really do exist).

138 • Don't ever be ashamed of the Gospel.

139 • Be careful of people who worship creation more than the Creator.

140 • The Ten Commandments are still in effect.

141 • Moment-by-moment true spirituality involves acting (at any given moment) upon the beliefs which you have as a Christian.

142 • Remember that The Holy Spirit is living inside you and he's there to help you.

143 • There is a seen and an unseen world.

144 • Everything that happens to you is for your own good whether you realize it or not.

145 • Moral relativism ("if it feels good, do it") is what most people use to justify the things they do.

146 • There are no gray areas with the Lord.

147 • Whomever you choose to marry,
make sure that he or she is a believer.

148 • Whenever you're having a problem, remember that God will either give you the grace you need to deal with it or he'll change the circumstances so you don't have to.

149 • Agape (Christian) love is the greatest virtue you can have.

150 • Don't believe people who act as if their denomination is the sole repository of God's truth.

151 • Set a good example for those who know you by being generous with your money and your compliments.

152 • Be proud of your weaknesses because they will cause you to rely more on God.

153 • Prejudice and discrimination should have no place in your life because they result from conceit and arrogance.

154 • Don't forget to give thanks before you eat.

155 • It's O.K. to be upset and angry at times, but don't let your emotions control you.

156 • Life's not always fair. Don't expect it to be.

157 • Wisdom and caution go hand-in-hand.

158 • So do knowledge and discretion.

159 • If you build your future on things that can be taken away, you'll never feel secure.

160 • As long as you are generous, you will always have more than you need.

161 • When you help other people, you help yourself as well.

162 • A prudent person overlooks an insult.

163 • When you become a parent, don't hesitate to discipline your children. It will show them that you love them.

164 • A gentle answer turns away anger.

165 • Keep a smile on your face. It's healthy.

166 • When you do the things which please God, he will make even your enemies live at peace with you.

167 • When you are kind to poor people, you lend to the Lord.

168 • You'll be better off being poor than to be known as a liar.

169 • Wine and beer cause people to argue and fight.

170 • You will never be completely faultless, but try your best to be blameless in your desire to do the right thing.

171 • Avoid people who gossip and talk too much.

172 • Your good name and reputation
are more valuable than money.

173 • When you have children, teach
them the way to go while they are
still young and when they are
grown they will not turn from it.

174 • A kind word spoken at just the right time is like apples of gold in settings of silver.

175 • When people mistreat you, do something nice for them. In so doing, you will heap burning coals on their head.

176 • When someone praises you, simply say, "Thank you." Nothing more is required.

177 • The result of being stingy is usually poverty.

178 • These two things are good to pray for: "Keep lies far from me," and "Give me neither poverty nor riches."

179 • Don't hesitate to speak up and defend those who cannot speak for themselves.

180 • Avoid self-indulgence. It leads to all kinds of misery.

181 • God has a time and a season for everything that will happen in your life.

182 • There are few things more rewarding than for you to enjoy the work that you do.

183 • If you love money, you will never have enough.

184 • When times are good, enjoy them; and when times are bad, consider that God has made the one as well as the other.

185 • Don't be too sensitive to what others say about you. It will give them too much satisfaction.

186 • There is one question you will never be able to answer: "Why do the righteous suffer and the wicked prosper?"

187 • Remember that the "little foxes spoil the vines." (Little sins destroy our lives.)

188 • From a distance, God is watching us.

189 • Before you were even born, God had already planned out every day of your life.

190 • Nothing will ever happen to you unless God allows it to happen for his own purpose.

191 • Thank the Lord for your blessings.

192 • Listen to Christian music.

193 • Read a few verses of the Bible every day. It's best done early in the day.

194 • Learn to meditate. You'll feel better and get more done, too.

195 • Eat a sensible diet and don't be controlled by food.

196 • When you're wrong, admit it.

197 • Don't envy what your friends and neighbors have.

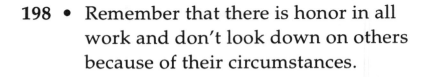

198 • Remember that there is honor in all work and don't look down on others because of their circumstances.

199 • Be sensitive to the Holy Spirit's leading in your life.

200 • Be a good listener and people will respect your opinion.

201 • Never give up hope.

202 • When your children come along, don't give them too much money. It will destroy their creativity.

203 • Be kind and gentle with everyone.

204 • Don't patronize places that sell pornography.

205 • Whatever you choose for your life's work, give it 100%.

206 • Whatever you do, do it with enthusiasm.

207 • Make it a habit to save part of every paycheck and invest it wisely.

208 • Don't ever let your children feel as if they can never please you.

209 • Don't let your children think that they can never quite "measure up" to your expectations of them.

210 • Low self-esteem is Satan's favorite weapon against us.

211 • Watch the movie *Jesus of Nazareth* every Easter.

212 • Have a nativity scene in your home during the Christmas holidays.

213 • Keep Sundays a special time for church and family.

214 • Call someone today who is lonely. The sound of your voice might just make their day.

215 • Make the care and nurture of your family your top priority.

216 • If someone sues you, make every effort to settle out of court.

217 • Always look for ways to make other people feel good about themselves.

218 • Someone once said that "Christmas is the day that holds time together."

219 • Guard your time with your family very carefully. It's the best investment you'll ever make.

220 • When you ask someone to do something and they say, "I'll pray about it," take that as a "No" answer.

221 • The real definition of success is doing what the Lord wants you to be doing at any given time.

222 • Don't measure your success in terms of money or social status, even though most people do.

223 • Be able to work with your hands. It is pleasing to God.

224 • Avoid people who give you "organ recitals" by telling you what's wrong with their heart, liver, kidneys, etc.

225 • Before making any major decision, make sure you are well rested and spend some time in prayer and meditation.

226 • Be willing to go the extra mile to accomplish your goals.

227 • Be careful how you act. Remember that you're someone's hero.

228 • Don't let the sun go down on your anger.

229 • When you're feeling down the best cure is to go out and do something nice for someone.

230 • Don't be afraid to tell your children, "I'm sorry." There will be many times when you'll need to.

231 • Don't withhold your affection from those you love.

232 • Avoid joining too many committees. They're very often a waste of time and besides, the Bible does not make any mention of the existence of committees in heaven.

233 • The friends you make while your children are little will be the most precious to you as you grow older.

234 • Love your mate. It's the greatest gift you can give to your children.

235 • Find a Christian physician to be your family doctor.

236 • Never forget the power of prayer when it comes to healing.

237 • Praise the Lord!

238 • Don't look down on unmarried people. God has a place for them, too.

239 • There will always be young people who look up to you. Don't disappoint them by careless words or actions.

240 • Remember that the mouth speaks what the heart is full of.

241 • Christian love and understanding should be your goal in dealing with all God's children.

242 • Filter everything you see and hear by asking yourself, "Where is God in all this?"

243 • Come near to Christ and he will come near to you.

244 • Make it your daily attitude to please the Lord. It is true that, "Your attitude determines your altitude."

245 • Go to a church that is alive in its music and worship.

246 • Be especially on the lookout to help an underprivileged child.

247 • Always try to discern if something is of God or of the devil. Remember, it is either one or the other, but it can't be both.

248 • It is important to hear God's word preached and it is equally important to act on what you hear.

249 • Even at those times when you are discouraged and you feel downhearted, remember that God is still there and he is not silent.

250 • Find a Christian brother or sister to pray with before making any major decision.

251 • Help an evangelist whom you believe is honest and sincere.

252 • If you start to accumulate too many material possessions, expect your relationship with Christ to suffer.

253 • Sometimes you will receive a blessing from a source where you least expect it. Remember that it is the Lord who caused it to happen.

254 • Be extra kind and helpful to persons with disabilities. God has a way of speaking to us through exceptional people.

255 • If the Lord gives you a profit in your business, take it and be thankful for it.

256 • When your children make mistakes, you must allow them to "pay the piper." Otherwise, they will repeat the same mistakes over and over again.

257 • See to it that you set a Christlike example for young people. You never know your ultimate influence on someone's life.

258 • Be considerate to a fault.

259 • Cherish your mate and make it your practice to do everything for each other.

260 • Realize that pets are another one of God's many gifts to us.

261 • Be generous to a fault.

262 • Before going on a long trip, stop and have a family prayer together.

263 • Delight in giving gifts to your children.

264 • Don't ruin today by being anxious about tomorrow.

265 • Remind yourself from time to time that the world's values and God's values are exact opposites.

266 • When something good happens to you, ask yourself, "Why me, Lord? What have I ever done to deserve this?"

267 • Concentrate on your blessings and don't dwell on your troubles.

268 • Remember that at Christmastime, it's really Jesus' birthday that we're celebrating.

269 • Be alert to God's creative genius working inside you.

270 • Jesus often went off by himself to spend some time in prayer and meditation. You should, too.

271 • Praise your heavenly Father for what he has done for you through Christ at Calvary.

272 • Eat a lot of whole grain bread and complex carbohydrates. It's the most basic food mentioned in the Bible.

273 • Don't be lazy when it comes to doing the Lord's work.

274 • Be sensitive to the Holy Spirit as he speaks to you throughout the day.

275 • Jesus had more to say about money and our use of it than almost any other subject.

276 • Make it a practice to look forward to your morning devotion more than the morning newspaper.

277 • Go out of your way to be kind to those with low-paying jobs.

278 • When making an important decision, remember that if the Lord is really giving you a green light you don't need to be in a hurry to commit yourself.

279 • Cultivate the art of conversation (especially with your mate).

280 • Don't watch the late news before going to bed.

281 • Don't pay your bills at night.

282 • Read a passage of Scripture before turning out the light.

283 • Let your last thought before going to sleep be the Lord's prayer.

284 • Try to be God's instrument of peace and love in the world.

285 • You will never achieve happiness by having more money than you need.

286 • Look for every opportunity to extend forgiveness.

287 • Pray that God will make you neither rich nor poor. Otherwise, you may have too much and disown God, or too little and be tempted to steal.

288 • If it looks "too good to be true," it probably is.

289 • Recall the story of the transfiguration and keep your eyes on "Jesus only."

290 • Your trust in the Lord must exceed (and be independent of) your understanding of him.

291 • Save a portion of every paycheck and invest it in a good mutual fund.

292 • Give your children all the help you possibly can to get started in life even if it means sacrificing your own needs.

293 • Never neglect to exercise your body as well as your mind.

294 • Your spiritual development is the most important (and most often neglected).

295 • Try to always make strangers feel comfortable in your presence.

296 • Respect your neighbors' privacy and try not to be a disturbance to them.

297 • There will be times in your life when you will be uniquely aware of God's presence. Cherish those moments.

298 • Try to be gentle and sensitive with everyone you meet.

299 • Evaluate people according to God's moral laws (which do not change) instead of society's values (which are always changing).

300 • Always look professional when you are meeting someone for the first time.

301 • Never, ever neglect to do that which you know in your heart would be pleasing to God.

302 • Be careful when signing legal documents and read the fine print first.

303 • People will always tend to judge you by whomever you "hang out" with.

304 • Lighten up on MTV.

305 • When you attend church, always give a generous offering. God loves a cheerful giver.

306 • Repay your debts on time. Your creditors will appreciate it and you'll sleep better, too.

307 • Get excited about something that will bring honor to the name of Christ.

308 • It is a good thing to enjoy great hymns. They're God's gifts to his family.

309 • Never hesitate to admit an error. It's a sign of maturity.

310 • Live within your means and write out a budget for income and expenses.

311 • Let your voice reflect what is in your heart.

312 • Tirelessly encourage those with whom you work.

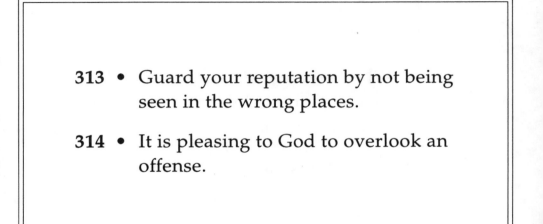

313 • Guard your reputation by not being seen in the wrong places.

314 • It is pleasing to God to overlook an offense.

315 • When you feel exhausted, spend a few moments in meditation and you'll feel renewed and refreshed.

316 • Learn a foreign language and be able to communicate in it.

317 • When you look at the moon and the stars, remember who made them. It will help you to keep things in perspective.

318 • Most people don't know it, but the Bible has a beautiful love poem in it.

319 • Let your speech be clear and concise, not filled with ambiguities.

320 • Don't neglect to prepare properly for a speaking engagement. There is no substitute for preparation.

321 • When disciplining your children, always be consistent. It will make them feel secure in the long run.

322 • A small amount of money given to a graduating senior is always appreciated.

323 • Give a Christian book to a friend on his or her birthday.

324 • Learn to appreciate good art.

325 • Be well groomed, but dress modestly.

326 • Whenever you see a rainbow, remember that it is God's way of reminding us of his promise to us.

327 • Make a regular investment of time with your mate.

328 • Don't buy cheap products. They're more expensive in the end.

329 • Try to do business with fellow members of your church.

330 • Don't associate with people who cannot control their drinking.

331 • When you pay someone a compliment, let it be sincere.

332 • Do not be intimidated by those in positions of authority, but give them their due respect.

333 • Don't let anyone discourage you from doing what you believe in.

334 • Have respect for dangerous animals.

335 • Be frugal in your spending habits.

336 • Never tire of doing good.

337 • Never fail to correct an injustice when you see one.

338 • Have a bold and adventurous spirit. You'll get more out of life.

339 • Spend every instant possible with your children.

340 • Cherish close friends. They are more precious than any amount of money.

341 • If someone asks for your help, give them more than they asked for.

342 • Protect yourself and your family from those who would harm you.

343 • If you are not trustworthy in small things, God will not trust you with big things.

344 • Try to see the other person's point of view even though you don't agree with it.

345 • The person who looks for trouble will always find it.

346 • Don't buy damaged goods.

347 • Remember that God uses prayer to change people.

348 • Don't flaunt your position of authority.

349 • Remember that the Scriptures tell us that some of those who are last now will someday be first in God's kingdom.

350 • Stay informed about current affairs.

351 • Don't hide your talents.

352 • God blesses those who prepare themselves.

353 • Three, seven, and twelve (among others) are Biblical numbers and appear over and over in the Bible.

354 • Learn all you can about growing a garden.

355 • Avoid taking unnecessary risks.

356 • Ask God to help you
find your life's mate.

357 • Remember Jesus' words about faith and the mustard seed. There is a direct link between believing in what you pray for and receiving.

358 • Try to forgive your friends when they disappoint you.

359 • Don't get intoxicated with alcohol. Instead, be filled with the Spirit.

360 • Don't neglect your spiritual development.

361 • Remember, we're not physical beings having a spiritual experience, but spiritual beings having a physical experience.

362 • It is God who is the Great Physician.

363 • When someone invites you to dinner, take a gift with you.

364 • Respect other people's feelings. They'll remember it for a long time.

365 • Take a food basket to a family in your church who needs it.

366 • Be a gracious loser and you'll always come out on top.

367 • Let your light shine!

368 • Take responsibility for your life and don't blame others.

369 • Break bread together at least once a day with your family.

370 • Gratitude is the longest memory.

371 • When you give a gift, make sure it's not cheap or inappropriate.

372 • A public library is a wonderful place to spend a day in a strange city.

373 • Never, ever give up hope for any reason.

374 • Don't be too severe when you reprimand. It breeds resentment.

375 • Be particularly careful with fire. It's very unforgiving.

376 • If you win, don't rub it in.

377 • Be able to keep a secret.

378 • Avoid people who ask personal questions.

379 • Support creative people.

380 • Don't neglect your rest.

381 • Be slow to speak, but quick to think.

382 • Honey is the Lord's natural sweetener.

383 • Get all the education and training you can. You'll be glad you did.

384 • Only give nice jewelry to those you truly cherish.

385 • Never forget where you came from.

386 • Be on guard against people who would steal from you.

387 • Everyone is hurting in some way.

388 • People are not responsible for their relatives' behavior.

389 • Be prudent with your money.

390 • Remember that banks are more shrewd in dealing with money than you are.

391 • Be careful what you touch. That's the way most diseases and infections are spread.

392 • Try to be the last person to serve yourself at a meal.

393 • Read everything and make sure you understand it before you sign it.

394 • Don't let your tongue control you.

395 • Set an example for your children by honoring Christ in all that you do.

396 • Have a humble spirit, but instill confidence in those around you.

397 • Avoid people who don't respect you.

398 • Take care of whatever God has blessed you with.

399 • Uphold family traditions and build on them. They'll draw your family closer together and will be a special blessing in difficult times.

400 • Look after God's creatures, great and small.

401 • Pray with your mate.

402 • Be a volunteer. It's the best work there is.

403 • Commune with nature. It's God's creation.

404 • Never underestimate the value and importance of touching.

405 • Have fun, but don't tempt fate.

406 • Keep your résumé current and up to date.

407 • Be spontaneous with your affections.

408 • Read the Bible over and over. It's God's way of communicating with you (along with prayer).

409 • Let your discipline of your children be firm but gentle at the same time.

410 • Be considerate of your mate in every way.

411 • Try to always be on time (or early) for your appointments.

412 • Smile a lot!

413 • Remember that Jesus was the happiest person who ever lived.

414 • When you fall in love, love that person with all your heart.

415 • Don't neglect personal hygiene.

416 • Fulfill your civic responsibility.

417 • Be generous to those who work for you.

418 • Don't ever forget that God really does love you!

419 • Pay attention to your dreams. They can give you insights into what the Lord's very best is for you.

420 • You can tell a lot about someone by the appearance of their eyes.

421 • If someone asks you to offer a prayer, make it brief and to the point.

422 • Be supportive of and pray for your pastor. Don't forget to pray for your pastor's family as well.

423 • Resist the temptation to share all your private thoughts. Some things are better kept private.

424 • If you lend money to someone, don't charge interest.

425 • When negotiating a business deal, don't expect the other party to "do the right thing."

426 • If possible, try to avoid putting anyone in a nursing home. They're better off in the home of a family member.

427 • When listening to a sermon, say this little prayer first, "Lord, what are you trying to say to me through this preacher today?"

428 • Be willing to pay a fair amount for professional services.

429 • A calm and peaceful atmosphere is best for raising children.

430 • If you are well rested, you will feel more optimistic about everything.

431 • Avoid being politically correct, and you won't compromise your integrity.

432 • If you know that you're going to have a really busy day, it's best to spend some extra time in prayer.

433 • Thank the Lord for already knowing what's going to happen to you today.

434 • Your minister is there to provide spiritual guidance. Don't hesitate to ask for help.

435 • Travel all you possibly can to other parts of the world. It will give you a deeper appreciation of God's creation.

436 • Remember that "the cattle on a thousand hills" all belong to God.

437 • Take care of the earth and everything on it. We do not own any of it, but we merely have the use of it for a short time.

438 • Once a year, make a list of everyone you need to forgive and ask the Lord to help you forgive them. Then, burn the list.

439 • When your children are away from home, cover them with an extra measure of prayer.

440 • If you're troubled by insomnia and you need to get a good night's sleep, concentrate on your blessings and give thanks to the Father for all he has done for you.

441 • Send some money anonymously to a family who has just lost a child, to help with expenses.

442 • Don't whine!

443 • When someone you know loses a job, let him or her know that someone cares. It will help more than you can imagine.

444 • Be willing to go out on a limb for something you really believe in.

445 • Never tell people that they've gained weight. They know it already.

446 • If you make enough money, establish a scholarship fund at a Christian college or seminary for needy students. Your gift will have far-reaching results beyond what you can imagine.

447 • When a friend loses a loved one, be with that person for as long as you can. Don't worry about what to say, just be there.

448 • Have great respect for the ocean. It can be very unforgiving.

449 • Once in your life, take your family to Switzerland. You'll be in awe of the beauty of God's creation.

450 • God is sovereign in human affairs, but that does not relieve us of our responsibility to obey everything that he has commanded.

451 • God will forgive you for any wrong you have done, as long as you ask for forgiveness in faith.

452 • Ask the Lord to show you what he wants your life's work to be. Then, trust him to direct and guide you.

453 • Don't be afraid to ask for help when you need it. It's not a sign of weakness, but an indication of maturity.

454 • Read Cal Thomas' syndicated column in the newspaper. It'll give you a Christian perspective on the news.

455 • Listen to *Focus On The Family* with James Dobson on Christian radio. It will be a great help in raising your family.

456 • Subscribe to *Christianity Today* magazine and you'll get a real blessing in addition to being informed about what's going on in the world.

457 • Beware of ministers who don't believe the miracles in the Bible.

458 • Give your mother a hug!

459 • Don't let pride get in the way of accepting help.

460 • Attend pot luck dinners at church every chance you get. You'll remember the food and fellowship long after.

461 • Give particular respect to senior citizens. They possess more wisdom and knowledge than you can imagine.

462 • Encourage your children to develop their musical talents to the fullest.

463 • Buy an American flag and fly it in front of your home on special days.

464 • Read *A Christian Manifesto* by Francis Schaeffer.

465 • Read *L'Abri* by Edith Schaeffer.

466 • Watch the movie *The Robe.* It's the story of a changed life.

467 • Ill gotten money will never bring you happiness, but right living will.

468 • If you are willing to be corrected, you have already taken the first step toward success.

469 • Listen to the advice of a Godly person.

470 • Remember that reverence for Christ adds days to your life.

471 • Let honesty guide you in all decisions.

472 • Don't spread rumors. Instead, be known as someone who tries to quiet them.

473 • When you are kind to someone, you are actually nourishing your own soul.

474 • In order for you to learn, you must first desire to be taught.

475 • Lies get people into trouble, but honesty is its own defense.

476 • When you are insulted, it is to your credit to remain cool.

477 • The real meaning of self-control is controlling your tongue. If you are too quick to speak, it can cause much pain.

478 • Try to associate with people whom you consider to be wise. That's the best way to get wisdom.

479 • Make sure that you eat to live instead of living to eat.

480 • There is a common bond among Godly people and it is good will.

481 • Don't drift aimlessly through life, but have a vision of what you want to accomplish.

482 • If you have a reverence for God, it will provide your children with a place of refuge and strength.

483 • If you have a relaxed attitude, you'll live longer and have more fun, too.

484 • If you have a lot of common sense, people will think you are wise.

485 • It will be better for you in the long run to be poor and humble rather than rich and proud.

486 • Kind and gentle words are like honey; they're appreciated and they're good medicine, too.

487 • Be loyal to your friends and let them know they can always count on you, no matter what happens.

488 • Never betray a confidence. If you do, you will find it very difficult to ever win back that friendship.

489 • If you ignore the needs of those around you who are hurting, you will probably be ignored in your own time of need.

490 • Wisdom is the most powerful thing you will ever possess.

491 • Try not to take pleasure when bad things happen to those who have been unkind to you.

492 • If you have faithful employees, reward them and let them feel appreciated.

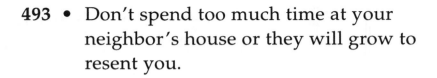

493 • Don't spend too much time at your neighbor's house or they will grow to resent you.

494 • Don't put your trust in unreliable people. The results are usually very painful.

495 • Don't spend too much time eating sweets or thinking about your own accomplishments. Both are bad for you.

496 • You'll be better off being hurt by a friend than flattered by an enemy.

497 • Just as a mirror reflects your face, so the friends you choose reflect what kind of person you are.

498 • People will always appreciate honesty more than flattery.

499 • Pray for those who hurt you and ask the Lord to soften their hearts toward you.

500 • Don't ever forget that I will always love you no matter what and I am praying for you constantly.

Scripture References

1	Mt	5:5	16.	Mt	7:1	31.	Mt	18:20
2.	Mt	5:7	17.	Mt	7:12	32.	Mt	18:35
3.	Mt	5:9	18.	Mt	7:15	33.	Mt	19:24
4.	Job	31:1	19.	Mt	7:24	34.	Mt	19:26
5.	Mt	5:34	20.	Mt.	10:16	35.	Mt	20:12
6.	Mt	5:39	21.	Mt	10:42	36.	Mt	20:14
7.	Mt	5:44	22.	Mt	5:23-24	37.	Mt	20:15
8.	Mt	6:3	23.	Mt	12:33	38.	Mt	20:16
9.	Mt	6:6	24.	Mt	15:4	39.	Mt	21:22
10.	Mt	12:36	25.	Mt	16:24	40.	Mt	22:37
11.	Mt	25:21	26.	Mt	16:27	41.	Mt	22:39
12.	Acts	20:35	27.	Mt	17:27	42.	Mt	23:23
13.	Mt	6:14-15	28.	Mt	18:4	43.	Mt	25:37
14.	Mt	6:19	29.	Mt	18:8	44.	Mt	25:39
15.	Mt	6:25	30.	Mt	18:18	45.	Mt	26:42

46.	Mt	28:19	65.	1Th	4:11	84.	2Tim	2:23
47.	Gal	3:28	66.	1Th	5:6	85.	2Tim	2:24
48.	Gal	5:22-23	67.	1Th	5:14	86.	2Tim	4:8
49.	Gal	6:2	68.	1Th	5:16	87.	Titus	1:8
50.	Eph	1:11	69.	1Th	5:18	88.	Titus	3:10
51.	Eph	1:17	70.	1Th	5:21	89.	Phm	:6
52.	Eph	2:8	71.	1Th	5:19	90.	Heb	3:13
53.	Eph	2:14	72.	2Th	3:13	91.	Heb	4:9
54.	Eph	4:26	73.	1Tim	2:2	92.	Heb	11:1
55.	Eph	5:21	74.	1Tim	3:3	93.	Heb	11:3
56.	Php	2:4	75.	1Tim	3:6	94.	Heb	11:3
57.	Php	2:14	76.	1Tim	3:7	95.	Heb	12:6-7
58.	Php	3:14	77.	1Tim	3:9	96.	Heb	12:14
59.	Php	4:6	78.	1Tim	4:8	97.	Heb	13:2
60.	Php	4:8	79.	1Tim	4:12	98.	Heb	13:5
61.	Php	4:11	80.	1Tim	5:1	99.	Heb	13:16
62.	Php	4:18-19	81.	2Tim	2:5	100.	Heb	13:17
63.	Col	1:9	82.	2Tim	2:7	101.	Jas	1:2-4
64.	Col	3:13	83.	2Tim	2:22	102.	Jas	1:19

• Life's Spiritual Instruction Book •

103.	Jas	1:19	122.	2Pe	2:9	141.	Ro	5:1
104.	Jas	1:19	123.	2Pe	2:19	142.	Ro	8:9
105.	Jas	1:22	124.	1Jn	3:17	143.	2Co	4:18
106.	Jas	1:27	125.	1Jn	3:20	144.	Ro	8:28
107.	Jas	1:27	126.	1Jn	4:19	145.	Ro	10:3
108.	Jas	2:5	127.	1Jn	5:14	146.	Ro	14:23
109.	Jas	2:17	128.	2Jn	:3	147.	1Co	7:39
110.	Pr	9:10	129.	3Jn	:9	148.	1Co	10:13
111.	Jas	4:7	130.	3Jn	:11	149.	1Co	13:13
112.	Jas	4:8	131.	Jude	:23	150.	1Co	14:36
113.	Jas	4:17	132.	Rev	3:16	151.	2Co	8:2
114.	Jas	5:5	133.	Rev	8:4	152.	2Co	12:9
115.	Jas	5:7	134.	Acts	7:42	153.	Jn	4:9
116.	Jas	5:16	135.	Acts	16:16	154.	Jn	6:11
117.	1Pe	2:23	136.	Acts	18:11	155.	Jn	11:33
118.	1Pe	3:4	137.	Acts	27:23	156.	Jn	16:33
119.	1Pe	3:9	138.	Ro	1:16	157.	Pr	8:12
120.	1Pe	4:8	139.	Ro	1:25	158.	Pr	8:12
121.	2Pe	1:16	140.	Ro	2:12	159.	Job	31:24

160.	Pr	11:25	179.	Pr 31:8	198.	Col 3:23
161.	Pr	11:25	180.	Ecc 2:10	199.	Ro 8:5
162.	Pr	12:16	181.	Ecc 3:1	200.	Pr 18:13
163.	Pr	13:24	182.	Ecc 3:22	201.	1Co 13:7
164.	Pr	15:1	183.	Ecc 5:10	202.	1Pe 5:2
165.	Pr	15:30	184.	Ecc 7:14	203.	2Pe 1:7
166.	Pr	16:7	185.	Ecc 7:21	204.	Pr 6:25
167.	Pr	19:17	186.	Ecc 8:14	205.	Col 3:23
168.	Pr	19:22	187.	SS 2:15	206.	2Co 9:2
169.	Pr	20:1	188.	Ps 138:6	207.	Mt 25:27
170.	Pr	20:7	189.	Ps 139:16	208.	Eph 6:4
171.	Pr	20:19	190.	Ps 139:16	209.	1Tim 5:10
172.	Pr	22:1	191.	Col 2:7	210.	Gen 3:5
173.	Pr	22:6	192.	2Ch 7:6	211.	Mt 28:6
174.	Pr	25:11	193.	Acts 17:11	212.	Lk 2:7
175.	Pr	25:21-22	194.	Ps 1:2	213.	Acts 20:7
176.	Pr	27:21	195.	Mt 6:25	214.	1Th 3:6
177.	Pr	28:22	196.	2Co 12:13	215.	1Tim 5:8
178.	Pr	30:8	197.	Ex 20:17	216.	Mt 5:25

217.	1Th	4:18	236.	Jas	5:16	255.	Ro	10:12
218.	Lk	1:31-33	237.	Ps	135:1	256.	1Tim	3:12
219.	1Tim	5:4	238.	1Co	7:27	257.	Titus	2:7
220.	1Co	12:10	239.	Titus	2:7	258.	1Pe	3:7
221.	1Pe	3:17	240.	Mt	12:34	259.	1Pe	3:1-7
222.	Lk	16:13	241.	1Jn	4:7	260.	Isa	43:20
223.	1Th	4:11	242.	1Co	2:14-15	261.	Pr	22:9
224.	Php	2:14	243.	Heb	10:22	262.	Mt	21:22
225.	Lk	6:12	244.	Ro	12:1	263.	Mt	7:11
226.	Mt	5:41	245.	Ps	100:2	264.	Mt	6:27
227.	Titus	2:7	246.	Ac	9:36	265.	1Co	3:19
228.	Eph	4:26	247.	1Co	2:14-15	266.	1Th	5:18
229.	1 Co	12:28	248.	Jas	1:22	267.	Php	4:6
230.	Col	3:21	249.	Eph	2:22	268.	Lk	2:11
231.	Eph	5:2	250.	Ac	15:32	269.	1Co	12:7-11
232.	1Tim	4:13	251.	Ro	10:14-15	270.	Mt	26:42
233.	1Jn	1:7	252.	Lk	16:13	271.	Heb	13:15
234.	Eph	5:33	253.	Dt	7:13	272.	Mt	6:11
235.	Col	4:14	254.	2 Sa	9:1-7	273.	2Th	3:13

274.	Jn	14:26	293.	1Tim	4:8	312.	Ro	12:8
275.	1Pe	5:2	294.	1Tim	4:7-8	313.	1Tim	3:7
276.	Eph	6:18	295.	Ro	12:13	314.	Pr	19:11
277.	Lk	14:13	296.	Titus	3:2	315.	Ps	23:1-3
278.	Pr	14:15	297.	Php	4:7	316.	Ac	2:11
279.	Jas	1:19	298.	Php	4:5	317.	Ge	1:14-19
280.	Mk	4:19	299.	Ro	1:18-22	318.	SS	1:1-8:14
281.	Mk	4:19	300.	1Sa	16:7	319.	1Ti	4:12
282.	2Tim	3:16	301.	Ro	12:1	320.	1Pe	1:13
283.	Mt	6:9-13	302.	Mt	10:16	321.	Heb	12:9
284.	2Tim	2:21	303.	Jas	4:4	322.	Ps	112:5
285.	1Pe	5:2	304.	Jude	7-8	323.	Eph	4:29
286.	Mt	6:14-15	305.	2Co	9:7	324.	1Co	12:4-6
287.	Pr	30:7-9	306.	2Ki	4:7	325.	1Tim	2:9
288.	Lk	18:20	307.	Jn	5:23	326.	Ge	9:12-17
289.	Mt	17:1-8	308.	Mt	26:30	327.	1Pe	3:1-7
290.	Isa	55:9	309.	Jas	5:16	328.	Isa	55:2
291.	Mt	25:16	310.	Ecc	5:10	329.	1Jn	1:7
292.	Mt	7:11	311.	Eph	4:29	330.	1Co	6:9-10

• Life's Spiritual Instruction Book •

331.	Pr	23:6-8	350.	Pr	1:5	369.	Eph	6:4
332.	1Tim	4:12	351.	Mt	5:16	370.	Col	3:16
333.	2Co	11:3	352.	2Tim	4:2	371.	Pr	18:16
334.	1Sa	17:34-37	353.	1Jn	5:7	372.	Pr	9:9
335.	Lk	15:14	354.	1Co	3:6	373.	1Co	13:13
336.	2Th	3:13	355.	Mt	4:7	374.	Pr	1:3
337.	Jer	5:28-29	356.	1Jn	5:14	375.	Jer	23:29
338.	Pr	28:1	357.	Mt	17:20	376.	Pr	22:11
339.	Mal	4:6	358.	Mt	18:21-22	377.	Pr	11:13
340.	Pr	27:10	359.	Eph	5:18	378.	1Co	13:5
341.	1Co	12:28	360.	1Tim	4:6-9	379.	Ro	12:8
342.	1Tim	5:8	361.	1Pe	2:5	380.	Ex	31:15
343.	Lk	16:10-12	362.	Ac	9:34	381.	Jas	1:19
344.	Pr	20:5	363.	Lk	10:5-8	382.	Eze	3:3
345.	Pr	6:19	364.	1Th	5:14-15	383.	Heb	5:14
346.	Pr	23:23	365.	2Co	9:11	384.	Lk	15:22
347.	1Ch	5:20	366.	Pr	22:11	385.	Ro	11:16
348.	Pr	29:23	367.	2Pe	1:19	386.	Ex	22:3
349.	Mk	10:31	368.	1Co	7:24	387.	Job	36:15

388.	Ge	4:8	407.	SS	1:1-4	426.	Lev	19:32
389.	Pr	13:11	408.	2Tim	3:16	427.	1Tim	5:17
390.	Ex	22:25	409.	Heb	12:7-10	428.	Mt	20:2
391.	Isa	52:11	410.	Jas	3:17	429.	1Pe	3:4
392.	Gal	5:22-23	411.	1Pe	1:13	430.	1Ch	22:9
393.	Pr	28:26	412.	Gal	5:22	431.	Pr	13:6
394.	Jas	1:26	413.	Mt	5:1-12	432.	Lk	6:12
395.	Eph	6:4	414.	Eph	5:22-33	433.	1Pe	1:2
396.	Ro	12:8	415.	Ps	24:4	434.	2Tim	4:1-6
397.	1Tim	3:2	416.	Heb	13:17	435.	Ro	1:20
398.	1Tim	6:20	417.	Ps	112:5	436.	Ps	50:10
399.	1Tim	3:5	418.	1Jn	4:10	437.	2Tim	1:12
400.	Ge	6:19	419.	Ac	2:17	438.	Lk	6:37
401.	Jas	5:16	420.	Mt	6:22	439.	Heb	2:13
402.	Ps	112:5	421.	Mt	6:5	440.	2Co	6:3-10
403.	Ro	1:20	422.	Eph	4:11	441.	Mt	5:4
404.	SS	2:6	423.	1Pe	4:7	442.	Php	2:14
405.	Mt	4:7	424.	Ex	22:25	443.	Pr	19:17
406.	2Tim	4:2	425.	Lk	16:8	444.	Mt	10:22

445.	Gal	2:6	464.	1Pe	2:2	483.	Pr	14:29
446.	Php	4:18-19	465.	1Pe	2:2	484.	Pr	14:33
447.	Job	29:25	466.	Mt	27:28	485.	Pr	16:19
448.	Ps	139:8-10	467.	Pr	10:2	486.	Pr	16:24
449.	Mic	4:1-2	468.	Pr	10:17	487.	Pr	17:17
450.	Ro	9:1-21	469.	Pr	10:21	488.	Pr	18:19
451.	Mk	2:7	470.	Pr	10:27	489.	Pr	21:13
452.	Eph	4:12	471.	Pr	11:3	490.	Pr	24:3
453.	Lk	18:1	472.	Pr	10:13	491.	Pr	24:17
454.	2Tim	2:22	473.	Pr	11:17	492.	Pr	25:13
455.	1Tim	5:4	474.	Pr	12:1	493.	Pr	25:17
456.	1Jn	4:6	475.	Pr	12:13	494.	Pr	25:19
457.	Ps	77:11	476.	Pr	12:16	495.	Pr	25:27
458.	Pr	1:8	477.	Pr	13:3	496.	Pr	27:6
459.	Pr	16:18	478.	Pr	13:20	497.	Pr	27:19
460.	Ac	2:42	479.	Pr	13:25	498.	Pr	28:23
461.	Lev	19:32	480.	Pr	14:9	499.	Pr	29:10
462.	2Ch	34:12	481.	Pr	14:8	500.	1Pe	4:8
463.	1Pe	2:16-17	482.	Pr	14:26			